SELF-DISCOVERY JOURNAL
FOR TEENAGE GIRLS

SELF-DISCOVERY JOURNAL

FOR

TEENAGE GIRLS

Prompts and Practices to Ignite Self-Awareness and Connect with Your True Self

Kimberly Hinman, PhD

ROCKRIDGE PRESS

First Rockridge Press trade paperback edition June 2022

Rockridge Press and the Rockridge Press logo are trademarks or registered trademarks of Callisto Media Inc. and/or its affiliates in the United States and other countries and may not be used without written permission.

For general information on our other products and services, please contact our Customer Care Department within the United States at (866) 744-2665, or outside the United States at (510) 253-0500.

Paperback ISBN: 978-1-68539-238-3

Manufactured in the United States of America

Interior and Cover Designer: Alex Klawitter and Alan Carr
Art Producer: Sara Feinstein
Editor: Elizabeth Baird
Production Editor: Holland Baker
Production Manager: Holly Haydash

Illustrations used under license from Creative Market and Pixel Buddha/Design Cuts.
Author photo courtesy of Anna Petrow.

10 9 8 7 6 5 4 3 2 1 0

CONTENTS

THIS JOURNAL BELONGS TO:

____

Welcome to Your Journal

Welcome to your self-discovery journal! This is a place for you to explore all the unique and wonderful parts of yourself. No matter who you are or what is going on in your life right now, this journal will help you get in touch with your values and goals. How do I know this? Not only have I been a teenage girl, but I work with teens just like you every day. In my job as a clinical psychologist, I help girls bridge the gap between their current selves and who they want to be. I've seen firsthand how guided self-reflection can improve confidence, bring joy into your life, and allow you to feel freer in who you are and what you stand for.

The journey to self-discovery isn't always easy. As you complete this journal, you are likely to discover things about yourself that may surprise and even shock you. That's okay and completely normal. My hope is that the prompts and exercises in this book will gently guide you toward identifying your motivations and fears, hopes and ambitions, challenges and joys. By understanding more about your true self, you'll be on your way to living a more authentic and meaningful life. Happy journaling!

How to Use This Journal

There is no right or wrong way to use the journal. Feel free to explore and express yourself however you like. You can start at the beginning and work in order, or pick a random page every time. It's totally up to you! There is no set schedule for completing the exercises, but you might like to set aside time each day or week. Even if you can't commit to journaling consistently, taking time whenever you find it will still benefit you. Think of journaling as a form of self-care. To make the experience as enticing and fun as possible, designate a special, cozy spot that engages all your senses. You could snuggle up with your favorite blanket, put on your favorite music, make some soothing tea or hot chocolate, and write with colored pencils or gel pens. Enjoy the journey ahead! You're about to learn more about your values, your inner thoughts and emotions, and the role you play in relationships with others.

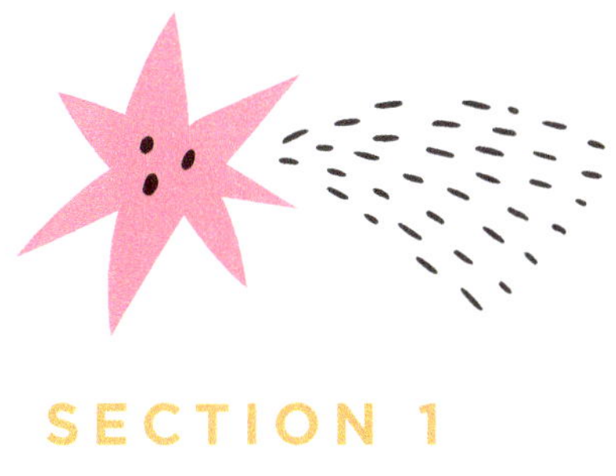

DISCOVERING WHAT DEFINES YOU

This first section is all about learning what makes you uniquely you. What drives you? What holds you back? What excites you? What do you love about yourself? What are you grateful for? The following exercises are designed to build awareness and pride about the inner workings of your personality.

Imagine you could take the place of any person in the entire world for one day. Who would you choose? What would you hope to discover?

You've signed up for the debate team, where you get to talk about what matters to you and what you believe in. Luckily, you get to choose the first topic to debate! What topic would you choose? Why?

Make a list of your top three favorite movies, books, and songs.
What do you like about them? What do they have in common?
Do they have a theme?

Movies	Books	Songs

Reflection:

> **"FIND OUT WHO YOU ARE AND DO IT ON PURPOSE."**
>
> DOLLY PARTON

Write about a time you felt strong and confident in yourself and your abilities. What were you doing? Who was with you? What led up to this moment? What happened afterward?

Rate yourself from 1 to 5 on the scales below, then answer the questions that follow.

| Dislike structure and schedules | 1 | 2 | 3 | 4 | 5 | Enjoy having a set schedule |

| Procrastinate on important tasks | 1 | 2 | 3 | 4 | 5 | Finish important tasks right away |

Do you describe yourself as more meticulous or carefree? How does this quality impact your life?

Besides basic needs like food, water, shelter, and technology, what is one thing you cannot live without? It could be something abstract like "kindness" or something more concrete like "my planner." How would your life look if that thing disappeared?

Think of a unique fact about yourself. Something that is special and distinctively you. Write it down here and describe how that fact makes you feel.

SORTING YOUR VALUES

Grab some index cards, sticky notes, or pieces of paper. Write each of these values on its own card:

boldness	independence	challenge
dependability	adventure	creativity
health	humor	knowledge
tradition	rationality	passion
fun	sincerity	connection
justice	community	compassion
simplicity	growth	honesty
self-control	openness	curiosity
responsibility	respect	leisure

Then write the following categories on three separate cards:

» This value is very important to me.

» This value is somewhat important to me.

» This value is less important to me.

Sort the values into these three categories, remembering there are no right or wrong answers and no one else will know how you sorted the cards. Once you have sorted the cards, remove all piles except for the "very important" pile. Now, if you could only choose three values to focus on in your life, which three would you choose? How did you choose your top three? Do they have anything in common?

Aliens from another planet have landed on Earth. You've been assigned the task of explaining our world to them. Using yourself as a guide, how would you describe humankind?

Rate yourself from 1 to 5 on the scales below, then answer the questions that follow.

Enjoy being the center of attention   1   2   3   4   5   **Prefer solitude**

Feel energized by people around you   1   2   3   4   5   **Feel energized by alone time**

Do you describe yourself as more extroverted or introverted? How does this quality impact your life?

____

____

____

____

____

____

____

____

Choose three adjectives to describe yourself. How did you come up with those choices?

INTERVIEWS

Pretend you're an investigative journalist. Your job is to interview family and friends, asking them the same question from the previous page: "If you had to choose only three adjectives to describe me, what adjectives would you choose?" Continue the conversation to find out how your friends and family decided on these adjectives. Do they have any memories or specific moments they recall that depict you as "helpful" or "energetic," for instance? Were the adjectives easy for them to think of, or did some take more time? Are there any themes in the adjectives your friends and family report? How well do they match up with the way you describe yourself?

There is a magic mirror that shows you your truest desire.
People stand in front of it mesmerized for hours. What would
the mirror show if you looked into it?

As we change and grow, we can have conflicting feelings toward our bodies. Focus on one part of your body that you love and appreciate. Maybe it's your arms that help you play a favorite sport, or your eyes that allow you to see beautiful art, or your feet that allow you to dance. Write a thank-you letter to this body part.

There are times when we fail to meet a goal, or when something doesn't go as planned. Describe one of those times and what you did to get yourself back on track. Or describe what you plan to do next time something similar happens.

"THINK LIKE A QUEEN. A QUEEN IS NOT AFRAID TO FAIL. FAILURE IS ANOTHER STEPPING-STONE TO GREATNESS."

OPRAH WINFREY

Rate yourself from 1 to 5 on the scales below, then answer the questions that follow.

Enjoy tackling new challenges | 1 | 2 | 3 | 4 | 5 | **Prefer sticking with well-known concepts**

Open to trying new things | 1 | 2 | 3 | 4 | 5 | **Do not enjoy trying new things**

Do you describe yourself as open to new experiences or preferring familiarity? How does this quality impact your life?

....

....

....

....

....

....

....

....

....

What are some things you appreciate about being a girl? Are there any things you dislike? What do you think it means to be a girl?

Take a moment to look around you and find three objects you are grateful for. Then, think of three people you are grateful for. Finally, think of three places you are grateful for. List them here and reflect on why they make you feel grateful.

Objects	**People**	**Places**

Reflection:

HEAD AND HEART

Art is a helpful way to connect with our intuition. Being creative allows us to get out of our heads and be present in the moment. Grab some paper and any art supplies you have, even if it's just a pen or pencil. If you have other colored pencils or gel pens, gather those as well. Draw a picture of your heart or brain—you choose! Now, think about all the values, achievements, fun moments, and personal characteristics that make up who you are. Fill your heart or brain with these traits and interests. You can make drawings, use words or quotes, cut out photos from magazines, or print pictures you've found online. Visualize what makes up this core part of yourself and is uniquely you. Have fun and be creative!

Rate yourself from 1 to 5 on the scales below, then answer the questions that follow.

| Experience a lot of stress | 1 | 2 | 3 | 4 | 5 | Deal with stress well |

| Get upset easily | 1 | 2 | 3 | 4 | 5 | Rarely feel sad or depressed |

Do you describe yourself as focused more on emotions or reason? How does this quality impact your life?

Think about how you spend your days. Does your current life reflect the values you've identified in this chapter? What needs to change so you can be more in line with these values? What needs to stay the same or be strengthened?

What is it like for you to receive compliments from others? If you had to give yourself one compliment today, what would you say?

"I WILL GO ON ADVENTURING, CHANGING, OPENING MY MIND AND MY EYES, REFUSING TO BE STAMPED AND STEREOTYPED. THE THING IS TO FREE ONE'S SELF: TO LET IT FIND ITS DIMENSIONS, NOT BE IMPEDED."

VIRGINIA WOOLF

We all have parts of ourselves that can be improved. These are called growth edges. What are your growth edges? What areas of your life would you like to grow and change? How can you make this happen?

What is a quality you admire about yourself? It can be anything! Try not to overthink it. Just focus on the first thing that comes to mind. Describe this quality in detail.

Think of a place where you feel safe and happy. It can be real or imaginary. Where are you? In nature, in a city, at home? Are you with others or alone? Describe as many details as possible. What is it about this place that makes you feel so secure?

WELCOME TO MY TED TALK

One way to improve our confidence in a subject area is to teach that topic to someone else. Think of something you've learned about yourself through the journal prompts. Perhaps you learned what you're most grateful for or what your most important values are. What was it like to learn these things about yourself? How do you feel after coming to these conclusions and developing these insights into your identity? In what ways has learning this benefited you? Take some time to record your own TED Talk on what you learned. You can share it or keep it for yourself. Just focus on describing these new revelations about yourself to others. Watch a couple TED Talks for inspiration and then press record! Don't worry about being too scripted. Instead, try to speak from your heart.

Recall your most recent achievement, something that made you feel proud. What strengths or skills did you use to accomplish this? How could you apply these strengths or skills in other parts of your life?

Rate yourself from 1 to 5 on the scales below, then answer the questions that follow.

Enjoy when everyone agrees	1	2	3	4	5	**Enjoy debate**

Enjoy when everyone wins	1	2	3	4	5	**Enjoy competition and a clear winner**

Do you describe yourself as more agreeable or as someone who enjoys competition? How does this quality impact your life?

Write about someone you look up to. Perhaps it is a parent, teacher, or public figure. What do you admire about them? In what ways do you see parts of yourself in them?

EXPLORING THOUGHTS AND EMOTIONS

In this section, you will explore the feelings and thoughts that make up your personal narrative. What stories do you tell yourself about your abilities, strengths, and weaknesses? How do these stories shape your identity and self-esteem? These questions will also help identify healthy ways of coping with negative feelings.

When has a friend or family member made you feel really good about yourself? What did they do or say that made you feel this way?

Emotional awareness is when you recognize what you're feeling before you act on that emotion. How do you recognize when you're sad, happy, angry, anxious, or excited? What thoughts do you have? What sensations do you feel in your body? Tingling? Warmth? Tightness? Describe your experience with these emotions.

Sad

Happy

Angry

Excited

Anxious

We all have an inner critic. It's the part of you that can get you down and make you feel like you aren't *enough*. But usually, these critical thoughts aren't an accurate reflection of reality. Can you think of more compassionate, realistic responses to your inner critic?

Critical Thought	Compassionate Response
"I can't believe I messed up my lines in the school play. I'm so worthless."	"I was feeling nervous. Everyone makes mistakes. It means I'm human, not worthless."

How do you know when you're happy? Create a happiness scale, ranging from 1 (mildly pleasant) to 5 (over-the-moon happy). Describe some things you might think or do at each point on the scale.

mildly pleasant

1

2

3

4

5

over-the-moon happy

We tend to be hard on ourselves when we make a mistake, even though everybody makes them. How do you treat yourself after you've made a mistake? What thoughts do you have toward yourself and others around you? Is this the same way you would treat a friend who made a mistake?

"BUT FEELINGS CAN'T BE IGNORED, NO MATTER HOW UNJUST OR UNGRATEFUL THEY SEEM."

ANNE FRANK

Try not to think about emotions as good or bad. Instead, think of them as pleasant or unpleasant. What helps you manage unpleasant emotions? Make a list of your coping strategies. They could be things like journaling, going for a run, cuddling with a pet, or talking with a trusted friend.

When things upset or hurt you, it's important to remember that others don't control your behavior—you do! Think of a time when you were feeling a strong emotion and reacted in a way you regret. See if you can uncover what you were reacting to and think of other ways you could have responded.

Emotions come and go like weather patterns. Think of your unpleasant emotions as a storm system. What should others expect to see and feel as this storm begins to approach? How about when it's fading?

DEEP BELLY BREATHING

Sometimes emotions are unpredictable and catch us by surprise. But one thing we know for sure is they are temporary and don't last forever. When you feel your emotions are overwhelming, try this exercise.

Find a quiet space and take a few breaths. Put your hand on your lower stomach to help you focus on breathing deeply. Feel your belly expand as you inhale and gently release as you exhale. Breathe in for four seconds, pause for four seconds, release for four seconds, pause for four seconds, and repeat. Continue doing this until you feel your body physically relax. Try to release any other thoughts from your mind and just focus on your breath. Notice how changing the way you breathe can calm your emotions.

There is no way to truly predict the future, but sometimes we act like a fortune-teller without realizing it. Can you think of a time when you felt sure something would be bad, only to have it turn out just fine? How did these negative thoughts impact your emotions and well-being? If you could go back in time, how would you think differently?

The negative thoughts we have about ourselves come from our inner critic. Take a moment to get to know your inner critic. Ask your critic what it is afraid of. What is it trying to protect you from—failure, embarrassment, disappointment? Are there steps you can take to quiet your critic's fears?

How do you know when you're angry? Create an anger scale, ranging from 1 (mildly irritated) to 5 (extremely angry). Describe some things you might think or do at each point on the scale.

mildly irritated

1

2

3

4

5

extremely angry

We unconsciously repeat our fears in our thoughts all the time. This unknowingly transforms those fears into beliefs about ourselves. Luckily, positive self-talk works the same way. Repeating hopes and compliments can actually help you believe them. Complete these affirmations with positive statements about yourself and your abilities. Try to repeat them as often as possible.

I can

I will

I am

I love

I hope

I deserve

I believe

STICK TO THE POSITIVES!

Grab some sticky notes or small pieces of paper and write 10 affirmations. These are short, positive statements about yourself. For example, "I believe in my abilities" or "My voice matters." Take some time to think about what you want to say. You can choose ones you wrote in the last prompt, on page 51, or write completely new ones. You can also look up affirmations to find ones that you connect with. Write each affirmation on a separate note and stick them throughout your home. Maybe one goes on your bedside table or on your bathroom mirror. Find various places that you frequent during different times of the day. That way, you'll get continual reminders of your strengths and powers from morning to night.

Take some time to reflect on the positive things in your life. What is going well? What is something that made you smile or laugh recently? Focus on how you feel as you write about the positives and notice how it impacts you for the rest of the day.

Sometimes we think in black and white and miss out on all the gray areas. Recall a time you used a black-and-white phrase like "They are the worst person ever" or "That was the worst day of my life." Now, try to find the gray—both the positive and negative parts of that situation.

Your body image and your self-esteem influence each other. If you feel unhappy about your body, you feel unhappy about yourself. Start boosting your body image and self-esteem by listing ways you can treat your body with respect. One example might be getting plenty of rest so your body can relax and recharge.

"YOU BETTER NOT COMPROMISE YOURSELF. IT'S ALL YOU GOT."
JANIS JOPLIN

How do you release your emotions? A good cry? Moving your body? Talking about it? Write about the ways you let out your emotions and how you feel afterward.

How do you know when you're sad? Create a sadness scale, ranging from 1 (slightly disappointed) to 5 (hopelessly down in the dumps). Describe some things you might think or do at each point on the scale.

slightly disappointed

1

2

3

4

5

hopelessly down in the dumps

EMOTIONS BOX

Sometimes our emotions, thoughts, memories, or sensations can feel too difficult to manage. Maybe you had an argument with a friend or learned some distressing information that really upset you. To help tolerate big and unpleasant emotions, create a place to store and contain them.

Use an empty tissue box or small container that you have permission to keep. Decorate the outside of the box any way you like. This box is going to hold emotions that can sometimes feel too big to carry on your own. When you're overwhelmed and you can't focus on anything but the intense situation, write what you're feeling on a piece of paper. Then, put the paper in the box for safekeeping. When you're feeling calmer and can think more clearly, return to the box and see what you wrote down. Then you can decide if there is room for problem-solving or if you need to accept and let go of it.

Accepting and validating an emotion, instead of ignoring it, can help decrease its intensity. Recall a time when you were experiencing a painful emotion, like embarrassment, shame, or anger. Now, practice validating that emotion by expressing understanding and empathy toward yourself.

What happened and how did it make you feel?

What can you say to yourself to validate that emotion?

How does this affect the intensity of your painful emotion?

Jealousy is information about your hopes, wishes, and desires. Recall a time you felt jealous of someone. What does this experience tell you about what you want in life?

Challenge yourself to view mistakes as opportunities to grow. Think of a mistake you made in the recent past. What did you learn from it? How can it impact your actions going forward?

" FAILING IS A CRUCIAL PART OF SUCCESS. EVERY TIME YOU FAIL AND GET BACK UP, YOU PRACTICE PERSEVERANCE, WHICH IS THE KEY TO LIFE. YOUR STRENGTH COMES IN YOUR ABILITY TO RECOVER."

MICHELLE OBAMA

Sometimes we "wake up on the wrong side of the bed." This is when we start the day feeling a bit off, and we might not even know why. How do you know when this happens to you? What feels different?

How do you know when you're scared or anxious? Create a fear and anxiety scale, ranging from 1 (a little worried) to 5 (terrified). Describe some things you might think or do at each point on the scale.

a little worried

1

2

3

4

5

terrified

What makes you feel stressed? Write down your stressors, then respond to them by validating your emotions. Finally, think of a way that could help you cope with each stressor.

Stressor	Validation	Way to Cope
"I'm stressed about tomorrow's test."	"It makes sense that I'm worried about the test because performing well is important to me."	"To help calm my stress, I can study hard for one hour and then get a good night's sleep."

SELF-CARE KIT

A self-care kit is great when you need a little pick-me-up or a reward for getting through a tough task. Perhaps you've been studying for an exam, or maybe it's been a rough week and things really haven't been going your way. Here's how to make your own self-care kit.

Get a container that's big enough to fit items like a candle, bubble bath, hand lotion, a greeting card that makes you smile, or a picture of your pet. Over time, keep an eye out for things that bring you joy and place them in your container. Maybe your reward is to look through old photos and memories of happy times. There is no right or wrong way to assemble this kit—you're the expert on your own self-care!

It's normal to have regrets sometimes. The important part is owning our behavior and learning from it. Write about a past situation where you had a response that you wish you could do over. What would you have done differently? What have you learned?

How and when do you reward yourself? Do you tell yourself something kind, watch a favorite show, or catch up with a friend? Make a list of rewards to use after you achieve a goal, overcome an obstacle, or just need an extra dose of self-care.

My Rewards:

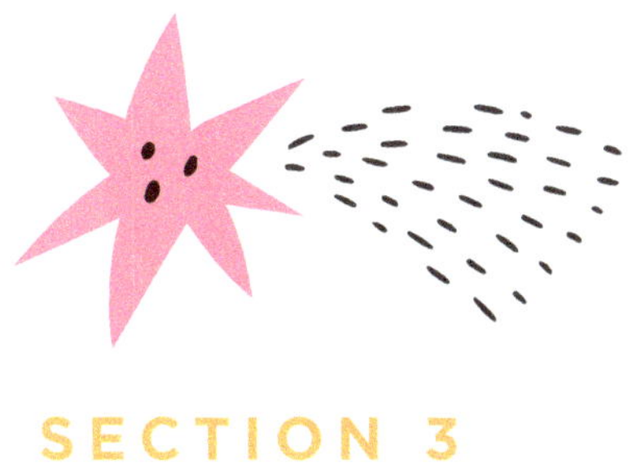

NAVIGATING RELATIONSHIPS

This section examines how you behave with other people. What kind of friend are you and what kind of friend do you need? It will also explore ways to connect with others through empathy, kindness, and managing conflict.

In group settings, we often fall into certain roles or patterns of behavior. What role do you play in your friend group? Some examples include peacekeeper, challenger, organizer, or realist. Does this align with how you see yourself and who you'd like to be?

When a friend, family member, or teacher offers you advice, how do you respond? Are you open to support and suggestions? Does it depend on who it's coming from? Who are some of the people you're most open to receiving advice from? Why?

Take a moment to describe your ideal best friend. How do they treat you and others around them? How many of these qualities do you also see in yourself?

"EMPATHY IS SIMPLY LISTENING, HOLDING SPACE, WITHHOLDING JUDGMENT, EMOTIONALLY CONNECTING, AND COMMUNICATING THAT INCREDIBLY HEALING MESSAGE OF YOU'RE NOT ALONE."
BRENÉ BROWN

How do others know that you love and care about them?
Describe the ways you express this. Maybe you get them a
special treat or save them a seat when they are running late. Or
maybe you tell them with words how much they mean to you.

When we're learning something new, we need help from others who are more experienced. How do you like to receive support in these moments? Can you recall a time you felt energized by learning from someone else?

A new student has joined your school, and someone is describing your friend group to them. What adjectives or descriptors would they use? Does this align with what you value in friendships?

Write about a time you had to collaborate with others. It could be a group project, volunteer activity, or a team sport. What did you appreciate about this experience? When did you feel closest to others?

MY HOME

On a separate sheet of paper, draw a house that represents your relationships with others. The windows and doors can be open or closed. Label each window and door to represent when you are open and when you are closed off. Maybe you're open to feedback from teachers but not from family or friends. Next, draw and label the pathways that lead to certain parts of your house. What are the steps people need to take to gain access to various parts of you? Maybe they need to build trust before you are willing to confide in them. If so, you might draw a "trust path" going to the "confiding room." There are no right or wrong ways to build your house because it's totally unique to you! Sometimes it can be difficult to express ourselves with words, so try using this artistic outlet to express your needs and boundaries in relationships with others.

Everyone has boundaries that define what they are comfortable with and how they would like to be treated. How do you respect another person's boundaries? How can you communicate to others that you are mindful and aware of their wants and needs?

What sensations do you feel in your body when you're having fun and enjoying yourself with others? How do your bodily sensations differ when you feel uncomfortable or unsafe with others? Use this chart to compare your responses.

Body Part	Sensation During Pleasant Emotions	Sensation During Unpleasant Emotions

Sometimes when we have unpleasant feelings about ourselves, we can push others away. Think of a time when others showed you compassion or empathy. What was the situation? How did you respond to their attempts to care for you?

Recall a time when someone close to you had an emotional reaction you didn't agree with. Perhaps they were anxious to leave, but you felt you had time to stay. If you could go back and empathize with their emotions, what might you do or say? How would that impact the other person?

MIRRORING EMOTIONS

Make a list of situations that would result in a big emotional reaction. For instance, learning that a household pet was diagnosed with a serious illness or landing the starring role in the school musical. Write each situation on a separate slip of paper, then put the slips in a hat. Next, gather friends or family and ask them to play this game with you.

Each player takes a slip of paper from the hat, then acts out the situation without using words or sounds. Your job is to mirror the emotions, facial expressions, and movements of the "actor." After mirroring and acting alongside the actor, guess what was written on their slip of paper. To help you guess correctly, tap into the emotions you felt as you witnessed your partner and mirrored their behaviors. This will help you build empathy and awareness of other people's experiences and perspectives. Good luck!

How do you respond to someone in distress? Maybe a parent had a long day at work or a friend is feeling down. Are you the problem-solver? The empathizer and listener? A mix of both?

How do you ask for support? Are you able to be authentic and honest with others about your wants, needs, and desires? Think about a time you held yourself back from asking for help. What stopped you?

What do you love about your community? It could be the friendly waves, familiar faces, or knowledge that you're not alone if you need help. Maybe it's your neighbor's garden or Sunday cookouts. Describe how these things make you feel.

"BUT PLEASE REMEMBER . . .
THAT NO PERSON IS YOUR
FRIEND (OR KIN) WHO
DEMANDS YOUR SILENCE,
OR DENIES YOUR RIGHT TO
GROW AND BE PERCEIVED AS
FULLY BLOSSOMED AS YOU
WERE INTENDED."

ALICE WALKER

Who celebrates you in your life? Think of one person who sings
your praises and encourages you. Write them a thank-you note
for all that they do.

Conflict and arguments are ways for people to acknowledge and set boundaries. How do you manage conflict with others? Think back to your last conflict. Were there any boundaries that had been crossed and needed to be reestablished?

Sometimes we feel pressure to act or look a particular way to fit in with others. This is normal—we all want to belong. Write about a time you felt pressure to change. Did any of the changes make you feel uncomfortable or go against your values?

EXPRESSIONS OF LOVE

A daytime talk show is doing a special program for Valentine's Day. You have been asked to join as a guest speaker to discuss love. To prepare for the interview, the show's producer has encouraged you to observe and take note of the ways you express love. Over the next week, try to be aware of how you show others that you care for them. Remember specific moments so you can share them on the show. Do you notice any themes in the way you care for others? Are there differences in how you care for your friends versus your family? Do these observations align with how you thought you showed your care? Or have you learned something new about yourself?

How often does your relationship with social media make you feel happy about yourself? How often does it leave you feeling depleted? If your social media accounts were a friend, how would you describe their relationship with you?

When you're assigned a group project at school, what role do you typically take on? Are you more of a leader, notetaker, organizer, or something else?

We can practice empathy toward others *and* ourselves. How do you practice empathy toward yourself? What are ways you can listen and validate your emotions without judgment?

"CARRY OUT A RANDOM ACT OF KINDNESS, WITH NO EXPECTATION OF REWARD, SAFE IN THE KNOWLEDGE THAT ONE DAY SOMEONE MIGHT DO THE SAME FOR YOU."

DIANA, PRINCESS OF WALES

Humans are social creatures, so we often fear judgment or rejection in relationships. But this fear can prevent us from being our authentic selves. Write about a time when you worried how others might judge you. Did you hold back from being your authentic self?

What do you appreciate most about your friendships? Reflect on moments with friends you are grateful for and how they have impacted you. What have you learned from them?

When was the last time you felt helpful or that you were supporting others? How did this experience impact your mood? Did you feel more connected to others around you?

KINDNESS CHALLENGE

Kindness is all around us, but we have to take time to notice it. One of the best ways to improve our awareness of kindness is to engage in it ourselves! Practicing empathy and helping people doesn't just benefit others—it also helps improve your mood. It's a win-win for everyone! Set a goal to do one small act of kindness every day over the next week. It could be as simple as offering to prepare dinner or helping your siblings with one of their chores. Or maybe you notice someone sitting alone at lunch and invite them to your table. After the week is over, reflect on how you feel about yourself and about your relationships with others. Do you feel any closer to people in your life? Have you been able to notice other acts of kindness toward yourself or others? Maybe challenge friends and family to do the same in their lives. Spread kindness!

How do you tell someone that they hurt your feelings or disappointed you? If it's hard for you to share feedback with others,
use this as a place to practice what you might say.

Strong relationships begin with shared experiences. When making new friends, what are some experiences or interests you like to share? Perhaps it's a sport, a genre of music, or even a new social media trend!

CREATING YOUR DREAM WORLD

It's time to put together everything you have discovered about yourself. This section will help you move forward in your journey toward a meaningful and purpose-driven life. The following prompts and exercises focus on making plans and setting goals for your future. Dream big!

You have a magic wand that allows you to view yourself
20 years into the future. Describe what you would see.

Think about the values you discovered in the exercise on page 10 (or complete the exercise now, and then come back to this prompt). Perhaps you learned that you value dependability. Make a plan for how you are going to act in ways that align with your values.

Value	Action
Dependability	Keep my commitments to others even when it's hard.

To make your dreams happen, you need to take action. Taking action can be really hard sometimes. One way to stay motivated is to break up your goals into smaller milestones. What is one small thing you can do today to get you closer to your dreams and goals?

Think about environments where you thrive. Are they filled with consistency and structure, or are they more carefree and spontaneous? What other features do you notice? Describe them below. Finding the right environment that fits your personality can help you succeed.

Pretend it's your 90th birthday. What are three accomplishments you hope to be celebrating with friends and family? These can be in any domain of your life—social, professional, emotional, or whatever matters to you.

Accomplishment 1:

Accomplishment 2:

Accomplishment 3:

Imagine your dream home. Where is it? Who lives there? Who lives nearby? What kinds of rooms and objects does it contain? What makes this home feel so comforting?

One month from now, where do you want to be academically?
What about in six months? One year? Five years?

"GIVE YOUR
GROWTH TIME."

LIZZO

Reflect on your spirituality. This does not necessarily need to be religious, although it definitely can be faith-based. What beliefs or practices allow you to feel connected to a greater purpose beyond yourself? How do these beliefs give your life meaning and purpose?

List three topics you are curious about. What do you want to explore and understand better? Maybe you want to understand global warming, a different culture, or how to bake the perfect croissant. What excites and interests you about each of these curiosities?

Topic 1:

Topic 2:

Topic 3:

If you were a brand, what would be your slogan? Think of it as your life's motto. What are the words that you live by? How do they help guide you?

My motto:

How does this motto guide me?

Take some time to think beyond yourself. What are your hopes and desires for your family, your community, your country, the world? What changes do you want to make in these areas?

HOW TO MAKE SMART GOALS

A helpful way to achieve your dreams is to make SMART goals. SMART stands for Specific, Measurable, Attainable, Relevant, and Time-bound.

Specific: Avoid vague phrases or generalizations, like "I want to be healthier" or "I want to do better at school."

Measurable: Instead, think of goals that can be easily measured. Perhaps you want to eat three veggies a week or have zero detentions at school.

Attainable: Next, make sure your goal is realistic. "I want to have straight As" is a specific and admirable goal, but it may not be immediately attainable. Try breaking a big goal into several smaller goals, like "I'll study for my next biology test for one hour each night."

Relevant: Your goal should be connected to your values.

Time-bound: Lastly, your goal should have a start date and end date. This helps you stay on track and holds you accountable.

Choose three of the goals you've journaled about and turn them into SMART goals. Choose start and end dates for each goal.

SMART Goal 1:

Start Date: ____________________ End Date: ____________

SMART Goal 2:

Start Date: ____________________ End Date: ____________

SMART Goal 3:

Start Date: ____________________ End Date: ____________

One month from now, where do you want to be socially? What about in six months? One year? Five years?

List three places you would like to travel. How did they make it on your list? What excites you about these locations? What do you hope to discover from these adventures?

Write your own creation story or personal narrative. How did you and your family end up where you are today? How has this shaped your identity? Include any details or events you consider important. Remember, you're the author of your own story and you get to choose what goes in it!

ENVISION YOUR FUTURE!

You may have heard of vision boards before. They are visual representations of your values, interests, and aspirations. They're fun to make, too! Pick an area of your life and create a vision board for what you hope to accomplish in that area. Grab paper or poster board, glue or tape, and any sources of visual inspiration you like—you can use magazines, newspapers, photos you've taken, or images online. You can use any words, symbols, or pictures you like! The only rule is to be intentional about what you put on your board.

As you create your board, use this time to reflect and meditate on what really matters to you. Think deeply about this area of your life. It could be school, a hobby, or something you envision for the future, like a career. What motivates you? What are your priorities? Let yourself dream and become excited about all the possibilities!

What is a quality about yourself that you really love and appreciate? Maybe it's your willingness to learn or your ability to take feedback. Or perhaps it's your adventurous nature or sense of humor. How can you protect and support this part of you so it can grow?

Imagine if you woke up tomorrow and all your fears, doubts, and concerns suddenly vanished. What's the first thing you would do? What kind of plans would you make for the future?

"WHATEVER THE PROBLEM, BE PART OF THE SOLUTION. DON'T JUST SIT AROUND RAISING QUESTIONS AND POINTING OUT OBSTACLES."

TINA FEY

How do you prioritize things in your life? What comes first and what can wait until later? Along with setting goals, it's important to also set priorities. A good rule of thumb is to prioritize time-sensitive tasks. Start with the hardest tasks first so you have the most energy to complete them! What are your priorities for today? How about this month? This year?

GIVE YOURSELF A HIGH FIVE!*

Change starts with small habits and commitments to yourself. By creating new habits, you actually rewire your brain to feel more confident in yourself and your abilities. Some of the biggest factors in success are consistency and accountability. Here's a way to get started: Give yourself a high five. Yes, it's that simple. Every day, give yourself an extra boost of self-esteem by looking in the mirror and giving yourself a high five. Can you frown when you look in the mirror and give a high five? It's pretty hard, right? There's something powerful and uplifting about it. By developing this habit over time, your self-worth can snowball into a more positive outlook on life.

* From *The High 5 Habit: Take Control of Your Life with One Simple Habit* by Mel Robbins

One month from now, what do you want your hobbies to look like? What about in six months? One year? Five years?

Your passions and interests are the building blocks of a meaningful and purposeful life. Make a list of your top five passions. Identify how you find meaning and purpose in them.

Passion	Meaning/Purpose
Fashion	An outlet for my creativity

" WHAT IF I FALL? OH,
BUT MY DARLING, WHAT IF
YOU FLY?"

ERIN HANSON

When we think about the future, we often think "What if it doesn't work out?" We focus on awful things that might happen to ruin our plans. Try flipping this by asking "What if it *does* work out?" Think of one thing you hope to achieve in the future. Describe what you will do if it all goes to plan.

Sometimes our goals become clouded when we try to meet the needs and wants of others. Girls and women are especially at risk of "people pleasing." Think back to moments when you prioritized the needs of others instead of your own needs. How would those situations have been different if you listened to your own needs as well?

COMBINING INTERESTS AND CAREER

Now that we've explored your passions and interests, you might be curious about what type of career this could translate into. Head on over to mynextmove.org to continue the process. This is completely free! You can search for specific careers if you have something in mind and learn more about the knowledge, skills, abilities, and personality types that fit this career. You'll also learn about the type of education that is required so you can plan ahead. Or, if you're not sure about potential career options, take a short quiz that helps match your interests to careers. You'll rate your interest in a variety of tasks, from fixing an engine to developing a new medicine. Don't worry if you don't have the knowledge or skills to do any of these tasks quite yet. Just rate how much you would enjoy each of the tasks if you had all the information you needed.

Imagining your future helps you solidify your goals. Come up with three jobs that you'd be excited to show up for every day.

Job 1

What would I enjoy about this?

Job 2

What would I enjoy about this?

Job 3

What would I enjoy about this?

We all have things we're good at and do well. Make a list of your skills and talents, no matter how big or small. Maybe you're good at remembering details or have a natural ability for mediating when there is conflict. Whatever it is, write it down here.

One month from now, where do you want to be emotionally? What about in six months? One year? Five years?

What has changed about your perception of yourself and others since completing this journal? Take some time to reflect on the wisdom you have developed.

"WE YOUNG PEOPLE ARE UNSTOPPABLE."

GRETA THUNBERG

Resources

***Ultimate Self-Love Workbook for Teen Girls* by Tabatha Chansard**
This encouraging workbook offers a variety of evidence-based exercises that are specifically designed to help teen girls build a loving and compassionate relationship with themselves.

***The High 5 Habit: Take Control of Your Life with One Simple Habit* by Mel Robbins**
Continue your journey with this book. It is a great resource for improving self-esteem and motivation.

***Don't Let Your Emotions Run Your Life for Teens* by Sheri Van Dijk**
This book for teens provides a more in-depth understanding of emotions. It also includes specific tools to help manage emotions so you feel calmer and more in control.

***The Power of Positive Thinking* by Norman Vincent Peale**
An international best seller that helps adults and teens alike learn to reframe negative thinking and create a positive outlook on your future.

***Atomic Habits: An Easy & Proven Way to Build Good Habits & Break Bad Ones* by James Clear**
This acclaimed book helps improve motivation and gives specific tools to build successful habits.

Let's Go Girl!
A podcast for teens by teens, covering everything from pop culture to advice on teen topics.

The Enneagram Institute
Log onto enneagramInstitute.com and learn more about your personality style by taking the Riso-Hudson Enneagram Type Indicator test.

My Next Move
Visit MyNextMove.org to explore career options that fit your interests. This website offers tools used by psychologists and career counselors alike.

References

Beck, Judith S. *Cognitive Behavior Therapy*. 3rd ed. New York: Guilford Press, 2020.

Carr, Alan. *Positive Psychology: The Science of Happiness and Human Strengths*. London: Routledge, 2011.

Clare, Maria, host. *Let's Go Girl!* (podcast). February 9, 2021. Accessed January 30, 2022. letsgogirlpodcast.buzzsprout.com.

Clear, Mark. *Atomic Habits: A Full Simple Guide to Break Your Bad Routines and Learn New Good Ones*. Scotts Valley, CA: CreateSpace, 2021.

Doran, G. T. "There's a S.M.A.R.T. Way to Write Management's Goals and Objectives." *Management Review* 70 (1981): 35–36.

The Enneagram Institute. Accessed January 30, 2022. enneagraminstitute.com.

Juma, Norbert. "Compassionate Empathy Quotes." Everyday Power. February 14, 2022. everydaypower.com/compassionate-empathy-quotes.

Kabat-Zinn, Jon. "Mindfulness-Based Stress Reduction (MBSR)." *Constructivism in the Human Sciences* 8, no. 2 (2003): 73–107.

Kim, Johnny S., ed. *Solution-Focused Brief Therapy: A Multicultural Approach*. Thousand Oaks, CA: SAGE Publications, 2013.

Linehan, Marsha M. *DBT® Skills Training Handouts and Worksheets*. 2nd ed. New York: Guilford Press, 2014.

My Next Move. Accessed January 30, 2022. mynextmove.org.

Peale, Norman Vincent. *The Power of Positive Thinking*. Mumbai, India: Sanage Publishing House, 2020.

Robbins, Mel. *The High 5 Habit: Take Control of Your Life with One Simple Habit*. Carlsbad, CA: Hay House, 2021.

Spradlin, Scott A. *Don't Let Your Emotions Run Your Life: How Dialectical Behavior Therapy Can Put You in Control*. Oakland, CA: New Harbinger, 2003.

Acknowledgments

A big thank-you to my family, my friends, and my editor, Liz, for all their help and support along the way.

About the Author

 **Kimberly Hinman** received her PhD from Columbia University after graduating Phi Beta Kappa from the State University of New York at Geneseo. She is a clinical psychologist practicing in Kansas City, MO, and New York, NY. In her private practice she provides individual, couples, and family therapy. She also provides psychological and neurological assessment in a group neuropsychological and educational assessment practice in Kansas City, MO. She currently lives in Kansas City, MO, with her partner, cat, and greyhound. To learn more about Dr. Hinman, visit drkimberlyhinman.com.